Discovery Of A Blunt Treasure

Discovery Of A Blunt Treasure

Bertha Blunt

Xulon Press

Xulon Press
2301 Lucien Way #415
Maitland, FL 32751
407.339.4217
www.xulonpress.com

© 2023 by Bertha Blunt

Contribution by: Abelard Alexis

All rights reserved solely by the author. The author guarantees all contents are original and do not infringe upon the legal rights of any other person or work. No part of this book may be reproduced in any form without the permission of the author.

Due to the changing nature of the Internet, if there are any web addresses, links, or URLs included in this manuscript, these may have been altered and may no longer be accessible. The views and opinions shared in this book belong solely to the author and do not necessarily reflect those of the publisher. The publisher therefore disclaims responsibility for the views or opinions expressed within the work.

Paperback ISBN-13: 978-1-66287-082-8
Ebook ISBN-13: 978-1-66287-083-5

To the memory of my parents and friends Ms. Lillian & Ms. Pearl.

Table of Contents:

Chapter 1 1
    Division Of Labor.. 3
    You Do It Before Me... 4
    Winning At The Begining......................................5
    Who Go And Where?... 6
    Butterfly On A Natural High...................................7
    Corny Ears.. 8
    Perfect Day For A Bug Out................................... 9
    When Depression Is Your Confession 10
    Just Me... 12
    A Time And A Line 13
    Trouble Exchange 14
    What's It About?... 15
    Holy Wood Or Bust.. 16
    Rag Us To Dust Hustle....................................... 18
    Pain Nurse.. 19

Chapter 2 21
    Cultivate Love's Garden...................................... 22
    "Un" Is The Only Condition Worthy To Mention............. 23
    Charity Till The End Of Disparity 25
    Spring Fever 26
    In Sin–Out 27
    Squashing Family Feud 28
    No Kiss Yet For Me.. 29

Chapter 3 31
    Inspiration Fixation.. 32

    Changing Times And Staying Times 33
    Strange Encounter. 34
    My Favorite Cheese. 35
    The Color Of Sound 36
    The Great Unload Before Bliss Road 37
    Exposed In Prose 38
    Where Is The Peace At Retail Beast?. 39
    Jason And His Peach To Keep 42
    Scourge For Jorge. 43
    Whooh Will Be The Life Of My Party. 45
    Birthday Agenda 47
    Tempted Again. 48
    My Wily Night. 49

Chapter 4 51

    Friendly Legacy 52
    Tribute To A Husband & Father 53
    The Breath Past Death 54
    Remembering Daddy 55
    Good Pain – Bad Pain Give Thanks Just The Same 57
    Some Go Without Saying. 59
    Foreign Purchase 61
    A Friend You Doubt 62
    You Are Not My Friend 64

Introduction To Bluntisms. 65

    Introduction To Bluntisms 67

Chapter 1

Division Of Labor

There are those people who sit and talk
Then there is the mob that sits and gawks
Then there is the last third, who barely have time to blink or smirk and are the people who end up doing all the work.

You Do It Before Me

Don't tell me what or how I should do.
There are too many willing to tell you and never enough who will show you.
I am not one to stand and bar a way.
But I'd much rather see you put it into action than to be bored by how you paint the air with your hearsay.
So, if you ain't got show to back up your tell
I'll just bid you a good day and I know you meant well
So, as I go, I'll keep on doing my best
And if I only tell part of what I've accomplished, I guess you can tell the rest
I feel I'm more comfortable hearing about what I have done
Cause honestly the more I'm told what I should do all I want to do is see how far I could run
Not meant to offend. Let's leave all offense behind
You go do the job meant for you and leave me alone to do mine

Winning At The Begining

When an individual or even a crew,
Has taken it upon themselves to pick a fight with you
Just don't flinch or even blink.
Be slow to speak even if it's not the way you usually think.
Let your flesh begin to shrink, Shrink, SHRINK
Don't be stubborn, proud or mean
Act like you have disappeared completely from the scene
See nothing and only hear what sounds right
Remember it takes two to fight.

Who Go And Where?

It doesn't matter if he go or she go
It's all about the ego
And as long as it don't go
Heaven will be a big no, no
Because ego is bound for the hell below
And if you didn't know before, now you know

Butterfly On A Natural High

I don't do bars; I find them too low.
And low is not a place this butterfly likes to go.
So, if you are headed for the bar, I'm sorry but I have got to fly.
(Alcohol is not this butterfly's high)
No, I won't follow you and I wish you wouldn't beg.
I just cannot picture me trying to empty a keg.
I fear if I was duped into that first drink and told myself each subsequent glass would be even more fantastic.
Then my once natural high would soon be a lie and the only thing that could keep me out of the bar sadly would be a casket.

Corny Ears

I don't trust being in this corn field, the ears are always in full bloom.
Shucked and always wide open to capture words meant for others in the room.
Yet when I attempt to engage them directly, they don't care to hear any of the words I say.
This usually leaves me pondering why corny people act this way.

Perfect Day For A Bug Out

When I was a young child, a cockroach crawled into my ear.
I was more than just a little afraid, and totally consumed with fear.
The doctor showed us the instruments he would use to fish the little bugger out.
I put up a fight, gave old doc a bite and let go with a couple of shouts.
He probed for what seemed like hours, he picked the insect to bits.
We were all glad when it was finally over, and I was exhausted from pitching my fits.
The doctor showed us the remains of the bug which he had smeared on a rag.
Mother gave an embrace; put a cookie in my face and said see now it wasn't all that bad.

When Depression Is Your Confession

When winter is upon us, the sunshine tends to be somewhat scarce
And the weight of our depression can be all the bit more fierce
The darkness lingers longer, and you wonder where is the light
Once the morning finally arrives, it still looks like it could be the night
I may not know why it is, but we are bluer during this season
However, this is the Lord's doing and I am sure He has a good reason
The months ending in -uary as well as those with -ember
We'd often like to forget, but oh how well we seem to remember
The bone chilling cold, shoveling all that snow and schools closed for the day
So many souls are vexed, though they find rest in knowing spring is on its way
Also, there are the Christmas and New Year celebrations
Just ponder on those lonely folks who receive no invitations
Are they worse off than families afflicted with cabin fever?
Each member believing there is a better place to be, a lie of the great deceiver
Why is co-existence so difficult for most families?
So close in physical proximity, yet so far away spiritually
Many other relationships suffer a similar fate
Our purpose here is to love, but some of us breed only hate
Should you find someone full of anger, filled with fear or living a life filled with doubt
With love you are rich and here comes the switch, to hit the blessing jackpot you must pass all of it out
I know God wants to use us, in darkness we are to shine our light
And lift each other's burdens not argue, fuss, or fight

Could it be that all along He planned this as part of His divine design? It's just a hunch, but during the winter months shouldn't we serve as each other's sunshine?

Just Me

Here's who I am. There is nothing to hide.
I'd be less than honest if I said a fearless child lived inside.
So, I stand naked and true.
Wanting to be free but unable to break through.
I am always thinking. Thoughts abundantly flow.
With more questions than answers of things I would like to know.
Then there are those feelings that sometimes feel like a plague.
Help is something I need often and I ain't too proud to beg.
Living life on purpose to connect with my destiny.
Why does contentment seem to be such a foreign subject to me?
On a planet where about eight billion people reside
How is it that I feel so lonely inside?

A Time And A Line

I thought I'd write a poem today just because I could.
It doesn't even have to rhyme to be considered good.
I don't have a specific reason as to why I penned this rhyme.
Other than I stopped to think and had a little time.
You don't even have to be an English grammar whiz.
A poem is a poem simply because you say it is.
Poetry to me is something doable by anyone.
All you do is to your heart be true and express it just for fun.
So, sort through your thoughts and scan your heart and write the words you feel and see.
And I'll be waiting and anticipating a poem that you can share with me.

Trouble Exchange

Jesus knows troubles are unfair
And you can go to Him in prayer
Bringing all your problems there
You just pour all of them out at the end of the day
And feel free to use your tears to help wash them away
Now that you have taken those trials to the Lord and He let you unpack
Get up off your knees in victory and don't you dare look back
All those things that have gone wrong, very soon will be gone
As for the issues you need made right
Faith will bring them to your sight

What's It About?

It's about family and it's about friends.
It's about beginnings and it's about ends.
It's about giving and doing it cheerfully.
It's about you and not just me-me-me.
It's about sharing a precious memory or two.
It's about coming together and finding meaningful things to do.
It's about exchanging a handshake or a warm embrace.
It's about forgiveness and extending grace.
It's about remembering loved ones who have passed on.
It's about lights, candles and singing songs.
It's about smiles and laughter and fellowship that's so sweet.
It's about all that comfort waiting in the meal we are all about to eat.
It's about anticipation of having something to look forward to.
It's about the joy of me celebrating the knowledge of you.
It's about something in my heart that I hold deeply and magically dear.
And possibly what's most important is that Christmas and Kwanza are just about here.

Holy Wood Or Bust

I planned a move to Hollywood
But did I expect everything to turn out good
Without first visiting Holy wood
For once I got there grace would abound
And I could take off running once my feet hit the ground
Then when Hollywood rolled around, what would have been sinking sand,
Was now a solid ground on which I could stand
I wouldn't have to fret over playing the lying games
Or getting a membership to the drug club to numb my pains
No taking up drinking to drown out my sorrows
Or losing my courage to face my tomorrows
I wouldn't have to run from a world that didn't make any sense
Since my stop in Holy wood gave me my much-needed confidence and strength
Now that I have the power of love on my side
I know my problems could never be answered by suicide
Abundant living and purpose are what life is all about
And when challenging days come, I don't look for an easy way out
I just be still and let my higher power fight my battle
And I stay off of that fence He told me I shouldn't straddle
Since I no longer blend in with the crowd
Even though I stand alone, I can hold my head up proud
When friends say, "Buy me!", I say, "Please!"
"I can't afford to, I'm still paying off my enemies!"
While Hollywood came with hoopla I didn't expect
Holy wood rained down blessings I'd never forget

So, if tickled pink sounds more appealing than down, out, and blue
Then my recommendation is Holy wood as the perfect place for you

Rag Us To Dust Hustle

I have a bittersweet story for you!
You can sit there if you want and act like it ain't true.
Yes, you eat that sugar today.
Tomorrow, it starts to eat you away.
Have you forgotten; we are what we eat?
Food should be healthy; life should be sweet.
How is dead food going to keep us alive?
We are addicted to junk; instead of what allows us to thrive.
Colored food was meant to add vibrancy to the Earth.
Strip out the color and you deplete it's worth.
Sugar goes so fast and the high is so fleeting.
When tempted to eat sugar on a diet, do you know who you're cheating?
It may start in your mouth, with your tongue and your teeth.
And it sure won't stop until you've reached six feet underneath.
A total melt down I can safely suppose.
Chopping down on your brain and then spitting out your toes.
Dust your house with flour, sugar, and fat if you must.
But you can be rest assured that soon that sugar will turn your house into dust.
The process can happen quickly, or it can be slow.
It tends to have a sweet beginning but can be a bitter way to go.
Sugar has as much power as the north is from the south.
Tricking you, addicting you and then evicting you from your house.

Pain Nurse

As I sit here nursing my pain
The anxiety is enough to drive me insane.
Oh, how I yearn to be able to get up and go
I feel the discomfort and tell myself NO.
It has been several months now I've been out of the groove.
Just anticipating the pain has me too frightened to move.
I'm praying and hoping it's a pain that has only dropped in for a season.
To be a permanent resident in my temple I don't see any reason.
Why I am here suffering I don't quite understand.
If I want to cast blame, do I point the finger at God or His man?
Knowing all pains are invisible are truly a mystery.
How is it that I can feel something that I can never see?
Pain, you better leave me alone.
You are not a property for me to own.
So, get get gone and bye bye bye.
It's the pain free life for me until the day I die.

Chapter 2

Cultivate Love's Garden

What is love? Do you know?
And if you do, would you tell me so?
Is love a person, place, or thing?
Is love high hopes or a diamond ring?
Is love or could it be, a gift someone could give to me?
Is love insanity or maybe Christianity?
Is love patience? Is it kind?
Why is love so heavy on my mind?
Is love something we should store upon a shelf?
Or spend it all selfishly on oneself?
Is love something we should freely give?
Without love, could we still live?
Now I admit, there is a lot about love I don't know.
But I understand love is essential, and we all need love to grow.
Some people think the demand for love is greater than its supply.
But that's not true and when I am through, you will understand the reason why.
It only takes a little love to brighten someone's day.
A gentle smile, a few kind words will wipe a multitude of hurt away.
So go on proceed to plant that seed; then you will soon see that there is no such thing as a love lack.
Just be patient and wait for the harvest, then you too can witness, just how bountifully that love will come back.

"Un" Is The Only Condition Worthy To Mention

Conditional love it is a sickening love
It is a love from beneath and not the love from above
Conditional love spreads faster than any disease
It's not a love that endures and all it does is deceive
Conditional love says you do "A", I'll do "B"
And on your death bed that phony love could be demanding "X", "Y", and "Z"
Whereas a genuine love says I accept the way that you are you are valued by me
Conditional love is not a love that can please
It says you got to be more than you are, but who are you going to believe
Conditional love says you must go a distance that would take you way out to far
Then leave you high and so dry for someone who appears to be better than you are
Then when you discover your treasure is up to only you to be found
Don't be fooled the second time those old conditions come peeking around
Conditional love is a game the world plays
Yet you won't win in the end, so don't you linger on that stage
The players can be friends, co-workers or even your mama
The stage can be different, but it's all the same drama
Conditional love is not what love is about
Just when you thought you fell in, next feeling to hit is total shut out
The wage of condition; a void. Who wants to pay?
Gives you nothing to hold and even less you can say
Conditional love is a love dead from the start

"Un" Is The Only Condition Worthy To Mention

Conditional love should have no space in your heart
So, if you want love, choose that which is exquisitely genuine
For this is the only love in the world that is truly divine
The love from out of this world sets up a standard against
Because the love of this world just doesn't make any sense
So, if the love from your past says you do or you die
Maybe now is a good time to give real love a try.

Charity Till The End Of Disparity

Public health is in demand.
It means that those with that power should spread it throughout the land.
Not with respect of person, give some and the rest you tease.
All you do with that thinking is spread around more disease.
So, if you're so inclined and you want to show you care
You gotta sow those seeds of love here, there and everywhere.
Not just for a minute or a twenty-four hour day
Not just Canada and Costa Rica, but even the good old USA.
See–If you neglect a hurting human, it's like you're saying they are not worth that much.
But what you fail to understand is that they will hurt everything they touch;
Including other people, the animals and such.
You cannot do wrong by a man or woman or even a boy or a girl;
Without expecting that injustice to have a negative impact on the entire world.

Spring Fever

Spring don't make me wait.
I endured a winter long and cold.
Make me warm and sunny, despite all those lies the weatherman told.

Spring don't make me wait.
I want this snow to melt away,
I know it's nothing more than water and it didn't come here to stay.

Spring don't make me wait,
I want to swim and ride my bike.
Oh, how I eagerly yearn to tell my boots go take a hike.

Spring don't make me wait.
The time to bear my winter depression is gone.
All life fresh and new is all my mind can focus on.

Spring don't make me wait.
Enough is enough already.
Temperatures need to jump, no climbing smooth and steady.

Spring don't make me wait.
The only positive thing to come out of the season getting ready to pass.
Is that soon it will be over, and all the people will shout
Spring at last, spring at last, thank God almighty it's spring at last.

In Sin—Out

You know I think you're a great person and I wish you could be the one.
But I'm afraid keeping our relationship a secret is not my idea of fun.
Besides I made a previous commitment with another man.
We exchanged vows with one another, and I feel I should stick to the plan.
Lord knows he is not perfect, nor the greatest man alive.
But I don't want to be the burden bearer for our marriage not to thrive.
While you have expressed your suspicions about the mate I chose.
Could it be that I made a mistake? Well, isn't that the way love goes?
Anyway, it wouldn't be fair to keep a tight lip about a man as special as you.
You need a girl who can tell the whole wide world, Lord knows that's what I'd want to do.
Even if we consented to put up a hush; and proceed to carry out the deed.
It would mean to excommunicate the one main person I really need.
He would know what we were up to although no one breathed a word.
Do you know where I am coming from, or do you think I'm being absurd?
You know this doesn't come easy for me.
For I once was blind, but now I can see.
Committing adultery with you is very tempting, yet it comes with a cost.
It means our souls would go to the pit, forever to be lost.
While you bring out the inner child in me and you know how she likes to play.
It sounds really nice, but at such a high price, I think she's gonna pass today.

Squashing Family Feud

Ebony has a grandson who goes by the name of Buck.
He often disrespects her, that's just a teen pressing his luck.
Buck's nanna calls him lazy, and this really gets his goat.
The slightest disagreement sends them at each other's throat.
They both have expectations, neither one has yet fulfilled.
It's a volatile situation, someone's likely to get killed.
Ebony said one day, she doesn't like to talk on the telephone.
Could it be because the caller would think he has just entered a combat zone?
Those two are occasionally subject to mutual verbal abuse.
Each one blames the other. How's that for a lame excuse?
Now I'm just an outsider, trying to put my two cents in.
But I'm a firm believer there is potential for these two to become good friends.

No Kiss Yet For Me

I'm afraid that I'd be somewhat remiss
To let our first kiss be pulled off like this.
It's just that for me and what I have in mind
Involves it happening at a much later time.
To include the essence of magic or fire that plays a part
Like when I close my eyes and see you in my heart.
Are you there yet? Please keep on asking me.
And as far as the heartland residency it should happen mutually!!!

Chapter 3

Inspiration Fixation

I love to attend events designed to motivate, encourage, and inspire. I be on a high all day long and even into the night. Then just before trying to settle down for bed – I tell myself the same thing at the end of days spent this way–- I say–"Girlfriend it's been another one of those days where you let yourself climb and dream. Now it's time for you to get down off your crazy high horse and go back to sleep."

Changing Times And Staying Times

Stop trying to make permanent, things that were made to change
And stop trying to change the permanent made things--- -
Take heed and be aware--- -
Don't forget the Serenity Prayer.

Strange Encounter

Are you a friend, family, or foe?
I am at a disadvantage because which one I don't rightly know.
Let us end the mystery and as you can see poetry is my game.
I'm a New York native, who knows what she's made of, and Bertha is my name.
Let's not drag this out, that's not what I'm about – I believe in keeping things short and sweet.
I thank God for this day, especially the way He gave us this opportunity to meet.

My Favorite Cheese

I just thought I'd take a little while
To spread my favorite infection, called a smile
As I wrote this mine was on my face
Now it's your turn to stick one in its place
Take that frown and turn it upside down
Those kinds of pusses no one wants to be around
A grimace uses more muscles or so I've heard
Don't smiling faces pass out good words?
When someone gets next to you, I mean under your skin
Look them in the eye and stick out your chin
Spread them lips and draw them in
You'll feel better, light, and tall
The other one will join you or hide behind his wall
If your smile appears to be an optical illusion
One smile beats two frowns is my conclusion

The Color Of Sound

I can rock a phone conversation any day or night and have the unsuspecting receiver believing I am a girl who's white.
Every word I say is very well received until I make an appearance and get treated like I'm some disease.
And to flip that same coin over I could be strolling in the hood and be approached by a brother or sister who thinks it all looks good.
And then they spark up a word and then I shoot out my reply as a welcome to Bertha's world
Only to be asked the question, "How come you sound like a white girl?"
And even though the question comes they don't seem to be really interested in what I could possibly say.
I think it is just supposed to buy them enough time to get as far as they could possibly get away.
Oh, can you feel my dilemma, I am a misfit whether I am seen or out of sight
And sometimes when I find myself alone, I wonder if I was meant to be a black girl or if I really should have been white.
But what if the whole situation got turned completely flipped upside down? And I sounded like a black girl and my skin was milky white instead of coffee brown.

The Great Unload Before Bliss Road

Happiness doesn't lie low.
You'll never get there if you follow the flow.
If you want to be happy, alone you may have to strive.
But both you and the flow will know as soon as you have arrived.
The low-lying flow will regret that you got to go.
They will be insanely jealous and will even tell you so.
But who cares if they spend years gritting teeth and/or clinching fists?
When you've just been granted your deepest wish.
It is a worldly lie that says it's up to your neighbor, siblings, children or maybe it should be your pappy.
But the universe declares it's up to everyone's intrinsic drive that can steer you straight up into happy.

Exposed In Prose

I once had an English teacher who knew me pretty well.
I tried to help a fellow student because I didn't want to see her fail.
We both had the same assignment; read a book and write a composition.
Well, I read two books and wrote two reports, my classmate put me in that position.
My teacher loved my book report, she said it deserved an "A".
She didn't grade the other one and she had this to say.
I know you wrote this for your friend the gesture was very nice.
However, she must learn to do her own work, or she will pay a price.
It is wrong to steal another's work, it is what we term to plagiarize.
I'm sure your friend is capable after all nothing beats a failure but a try.
I hope you learned your lesson; this particular incident I am willing to overlook.
If you really want to assist your girlfriend, take her to the library and help her pick out a book.

Where Is The Peace At Retail Beast?

I thought everything would be okay.
To take a part time job for the holiday.
The extra money would help me pay for my Christmas feast.
So, I landed a sales associate position at Retail Beast.
I figured things would be as easy as pie.
But there is more to retail than meets the eye.
Markdowns and fitting rooms are among the bigger tasks.
I used to wonder how those things got done, now I'm so sorry that I asked.
Everything started out just as smooth as cream.
However, yesterday, for me anyway, was like something out of a bad dream.
It was one of their super sales.
Many shopped with coupons, never fails.
All day long customers come and go.
Hoping you can help them with the things they don't know.
Where is this and where is that?
If this doesn't fit, can I bring it back?
Some customers get in line and wait till you hit the scanning gun trigger.
Their eyes light up as they compute their own figures.
Some of them I swear are on a war path.
Why do we use a POS terminal? Just let the customers do the math.
They want boxes, stuffed animals, and shopping bags.
Never a dull moment, time never drags.
It is a job that can stress you out if you let it.

The extra cash you can earn eases the pain when you get in on those express credits.
Most customers have sweet dispositions and a positive attitude.
Let's not leave out the handful on a mission to be downright rude.
One of the latter had the nerve to say,
"Why isn't everything on sale today?"
I fought the urge to tell him, "Hey, why the hell don't we just give it all away!"
What is the matter with people, we are not here to be playing games.
If you want everything in the store to be on sale you need to shop at Coldoors or FAmes.
Tis the season to be hectic, but I thought I had what it would take.
Not that I am perfect, I make my share of mistakes.
Most merchandise has sensors and maybe one I missed.
For that there was a penalty of being put on securities screw up list.
Not a major problem, no real gain or loss.
You'll just get a friendly reminder to take future security tags off.
These events just scratched the surface of my skin, guess what got underneath?
Trying to get a day off work was harder than pulling hens' teeth.
I thought I would be able to hold out.
One week till Christmas and I started to doubt.
I had a dinner to attend with my man.
It was well in advance that we made the plan.
I told my supervisor the situation and she said she would oblige.
But when that week's schedule showed up, what do you know---do you think she even tried.
Some friends were traveling all the way from Ohio.
And I'll miss out on this quality time because my manager said no.
Do you think that that's how my story is going to go?
Well, my friend, please think again because I for one don't think so.
I asked my co-workers to swap a day with me,
But none were willing to let it be.
Angel had a previous commitment, Lisa and Lil said no outright.
Sandra and Sunny have finals and must study that night.

Amanda and Betty are scheduled to work themselves.
What to do next, I'm in a fix, because I cannot think of anyone else.
It was after the fact that I learned the trick.
Never request a day off just call out sick.
I wanted to be part of the Retail Beast family for very long.
But if I put my job before my friends and family, I'm sorry it would be wrong.
I will ask Patty one more time,
If she would help resolve this conflict of mine.
If she is reluctant, then I will retort
To the call out line as a last resort.
I will punch up the digits and then I will say,
"This is Ms. Blunt---and I was on my way!!!
I just paused to call to wish you a blessed day.
And since this is the Sunday, you wouldn't let me get--- -
Merry Christmas to you all---OH by the way, I QUIT!!!"

Jason And His Peach To Keep

Jason is in love. And me he can't get enough.
No matter what I give him, he always wants more stuff.
He plays shy and quiet, just like a little mouse.
And he is always asking his mommy if we can go to Bertha's house.
It's nice to be liked, I hope this feeling lasts.
He imagines a nation of amazons, just like me.
I can tell by the way he smiles when he looks at me, through a magnifying glass.

Scourge For Jorge

Whatever happened to innocence? The unimaginable thing was did.
How was it that I was taken advantage of by a smooth talking seven-year-old kid?
With a sweetness and meekness, he approached me and offered me an embrace.
I was suspicious at first but accepted humbly with a big Kool-Aid smile on my face.
Then came the line and my heart was inclined to initially reject the bait.
But I later reconsidered, if only I had followed my mind which said, "Bertha, why don't you wait?"
I don't mean to complain or give Satan any vain glory.
The scam was full of deception, I should have never bought his story.
He told me his mommy gave him a party but neglected to give him a birthday card.
Now though I did not know everything about his mother, I did find believing this a little bit hard.
So, I told him to let his aunt know and then tell me what she had to say.
She paid little attention to his plea, and I watched him walk away.
He approached me again to tell me his aunt did not respond to him.
Your aunt and mom should know better, and I reassured him that I would have a little talk with them.
So, I retold the information to them and discovered that only two thirds of the story was true.
I told his mother, I was going to get her son and said make sure that you tell him to.
I considered a belt, but his tender skin might be subject to bruise, bleed, or tear.

So, I'll tell him why it is ugly to lie, then I'll lift his name up in prayer.

Whooh Will Be The Life Of My Party

Mom and Dad, my party is going to be really great.
Whooh and me can hardly wait.
I will be celebrating another year, making this my seventh one.
A small group will be coming together to make sure it will be lots of fun.
Dancing, games, and sharing photos are a few of the things we plan to do.
And in the spirit of friendly competition some games will be played for a prize or two.
Today is the day we've be waiting for---let's get this party started right.
Everything is just about in its place, but no birthday girl in sight.
The birthday girl is in her room getting into her party dress.
When suddenly the doorbell rings---must be the first party guest.
The food is smelling quite delicious.
As it gets put into the serving dishes.
The macaroni with cheese in,
Has turned out to be quite pleasing.
The chicken cooked on the barbecue
Didn't come with instructions; but we knew what to do.
The punch was spiced with cinnamon stick.
But that did not stop us from getting to the bottom of it.
Dorwanda made the Ziti
A cousin who is always a sweetie.
Yaya made two dishes one of which was the stuffing.
She is such a terrific cook, and she only does a little fussing.
It's time to sing Happy Birthday and everyone gathered around.

It might not be a chorus, but everyone made a sound.
The theme of the party was none other than our friend Cubby Whooh.
Whooh was on the plates, napkins, cups, and he was pictured on the birthday cake too.
Whooh started out a whole honey bear, but by the time it was all said and done. We reduced a 36-inch bear right down to a crumb.

Birthday Agenda

So, your birthday's rolling around again.
Will you be spending it alone or with a couple of friends?
Disco dancing with cake and champagne?
Out on the beach, but what if it rains?
Will you head it in early or hang way past eight?
I know you are not gonna pass up this opportunity to celebrate.
You have looked forward to this day.
What are you going to do, time is slipping away?
You are at an age that's ripe and hardy.
I know it's short notice, but I can throw you a party.
We know the day – here's the time and address.
Bring an appetite and let me handle the rest.
I know the foods you like---dress code something cute.
But if that one starts to boggle your mind; just show up in your birthday suit.

Tempted Again

Temptation in my way again.
Am I God's enemy if I give in?
Guilt eating me up, I can barely sleep.
I am in way too deep; why does the flesh have to be so darn weak?
Is it right not to do,
The things I often think I ought to.
It's enough to drive a sane woman mad
What I think would be good, I'm told it is bad
Denied access at Heaven's gate
Because of some forbidden fruit I ate
Idle worship I should forgo
But I seem to get caught up in the flow
Possessing a thought, I shouldn't have
Finding myself on that spiritual war path
I should be a brave warrior and fight the good fight
Or maybe surrender to temptation for just one more night.

My Wily Night

On many occasions you asked me if I would dream about you.
Well last night for the first time, I did what you asked me to.
Guess what? I was right there with you. I hope that that was okay.
It was a dream that I wouldn't mind living, I wish it will come true one day.
I forgot some of the details. However, there was a bedroom scene.
I followed you to the shower and watched you disappear into the steam.
You massaged me gently with scented body oil. You kissed me so passionately.
You know you had me tweaked.
I haven't the foggiest clue where we were; nor can I recall the day of the week.
I was just so glad to be with you, getting ready for some awesome love.
Yet something hindered my response. I don't know maybe there was something I was afraid of.
You looked into my eyes and said, "Relax baby, I don't mean you any harm."
You promised not to take advantage of me and then held me tightly in your arms.
In an attempt to comfort me you asked, "Do you think the timing is wrong?"
You said, "It's not a game, we both feel the same and have already waited too long."
I finally conceded, thinking it is possible that this could turn out all right.
Please don't hurt me was my plea and I requested you turn out the light.
As you reached for the lamp on the nightstand, you knocked over a coffee cup.
And then!!!---I wish I could tell you for it was at that very moment I woke up.

Chapter 4

Friendly Legacy

My Deacon / my brother / my friend
Is this really a beginning or is it really an end?
You were a husband, a father, and a brother.
Like you there will never be another.
When it came to life you knew how to live
And no matter what anyone asked if you had it you would so cheerfully give.
If ever I needed something I'd never hesitate to call you and ask
And even if your wife would say brother ain't going for that – you would be up for the task.
And every day wasn't cake and ice cream, when the mood hit, we would act like we knew how to fight.
I'd say something that caught you off guard and you'd give me your classic impersonation of a deer caught in a headlight.
Well today I'm glad that you made it home safe.
Even though behind you – you left in many hearts an empty space.
Goodbye is not what I came to say, it's a word I don't even care to own.
I came to thank God for the opportunity to have known you and to say I'll see you when I get home.

Tribute To A Husband & Father

If ever there was a young man, who desired to see a future brighter than his past.
Determined to be there for his wife and children until he breathed his last.
A journey though not always easy and seemed uphill sometimes.
Jimmy did not let that deter him because he was willing to climb.
He would take on the highest mountain, swim the widest sea, wrestle a fleet of gators to provide for his children because he equally loved all his family.
He poured his love into his family and their hearts could barely contain all that was pumped in.
And every chance Jim's wife and children got right up until the end, they poured that love back into the world, especially back into him.

The Breath Past Death

We were so sorry you had to go.
Understanding why---will we ever know?
It's like life – one day you slip in – the next thing you're out.
Who says this is what loving, and living is all about?
Who gives death his reign to assign and roll call?
Leaving behind survivors to deal with a void yay deep and about yay tall.
Some left without warning or the slightest clue.
And even though we keep going---we ponder HOW without you.
But just in case you thought you were slick enough to slip completely away.
You can try again tomorrow, but we remember you today.
We cling to the hope that when all days blend into one.
No past days' grief and pain can compare to that day's fun
All heartache, sorrow, and yearning will past.
We will see death transgress into eternal life at last.

Remembering Daddy

Whenever my daddy was around, we could always rip and run.
He taught me how to laugh and love – live life to the fullest, nothing wrong with a little fun.
There were some pains, some tears and life could not be complete without a few mistakes.
But my daddy helped me to grow strong, so I could get along and have what it would take.
He had a sense of humor that was contagious to say the very least.
My father was a wise man who knew the value in holding your peace.
A quiet demeanor he carefully selected as his usual way.
And since he did not say much, it was easy to remember the things that he did have to say.
He placed a high priority on family closeness, and he sowed an abundance of care.
No matter where family members moved, he endured the miles and made his way up, down, in, out, around, or over there.
He sure enjoyed his relatives and did not have much time for looking for friends.
He was careful to avoid forming rifts and was never too proud to initiate making amends.
I recall my daddy telling someone one day, "That ole Bertha, she sure is smart"
I don't know if I let on that I heard that one or not, but I sure did take it to heart.
I don't remember exactly what was so special that day that I did or may have said.

But ever since that day of many yesterdays passed, those words to this day still softly ring in my head.

There are other words ringing in the store of my heart and my mind.

And although there were occasions personalities conflicted, I cannot recall a word that my daddy spoke that was ever unkind.

"Didn't I tell you; didn't I tell you?" was what I heard when I did what I wasn't supposed to.

Now my daddy is gone, and it is up to me to carry on and continue to do the things he taught me to do.

As part of most children's play, they would contemplate the day, when they are free to live the life, they plan to have.

Well, I remember as a little girl dressing up on several occasions and making believe I was my dad.

Looking back, I believe that was my way of feeling that more people on the planet should be like him.

That would get out of my way, do whatever I say and love me whether I was good or mean to them.

I can live out the rest of my years with fond memories, tears, and examples of how daddy found his way.

I thank God for my daddy and the part he played in my life, making the contributions and sacrifices, so I could be the woman I am today.

Good Pain – Bad Pain Give Thanks Just The Same

Mother suffered a special pain once upon a time, it was near the middle of June.
The pain she exclaimed was somewhat severe, but it was expected to be over soon.
She had quite a few months to prepare for this pain. The avoidance of which was minimal.
It took three agonizing days before that pain finally–--I don't know if I should say for it to come or for it to go.
Most pains in the body are concealed and are not on display to see.
But you all have witnessed this particular pain, because just so happens it turned out to be me.
Since I was born in June that means most likely I was conceived sometime in September.
Whenever I displeased mother, those labor pains she would conveniently remember.
I remember one particular day; mother was steaming for sure.
I let her vent but decided I didn't want to hear about the 36-hour labor ordeal anymore.
I said how I felt with attitude, but if I am going to tell it I may as well tell it true.
I said, "Your labor was such as it was because I didn't want to be born, but you had to go and push the issue!"
It bothered me to think that I could hurt someone I loved so much.
Is it possible for a love to exist, one a pain could never ever touch?

My mother was one of those parents who desired to see her children excel. Now that is what you call love.
I did not feel the need to be better than mother, if I could be half the woman she was.
Then came the day mother passed away more than 23 years ago now.
I, at times find myself pondering if I was worth that pain somehow.
Also, I wonder if mother had a clue, that the day she left me, that I'd have a pain to contend with too.
I wish I could have had been given three days and have had this horrible grieving pain been through.
Living here without her is the hardest thing I've ever had to do.

Some Go Without Saying

I tried to say goodbye before, but you sort of stuck your foot in the door instead of leaving it be.
It may have a familiar ring, after all it was you who prolonged this thing by calling again on me.
I sent you a letter or even better for the style flowed just like prose.
It was sugar coated; after all I wrote it yet still you turned up your nose.
I got no satisfaction with your reaction, why did you feel my mission was to diss?
We should have let it be, I told you it was uncomfortable for me and too much confusion was in the midst.
I felt some shame after your claim that my words struck a nerve and caused you to suffer some stress.
Well, I was hurting too, because I really liked you and thought to myself, what a mess.
I thought we were strong enough and equipped with the right stuff and could leave this thing alone.
Yet lo and behold, history being told one day you punched up my digits on your phone.
I never would have surmised; it came as quite the surprise one cool autumn night.
You spoke my name as if things were still the same and asked if calling me would be alright.
I said okay but knew deep down one day we would reach our inevitable end.
And though we don't have closure, here lies the exposure that I will always be your friend.
I guess all is well to be able to live and tell how the good old days were served.

Oh, by the way, what would you have to say, if I asked, "Do you think I got what I deserved?"

I would never and I mean ever do that to anyone is an age-old adage with me. Are you a defeated fighter, if you listen to the song writer, who said, "Whatever will be will be?"

Your pardon I beg, although I would never have pegged you to be that type of guy.

You know the kind that seem to have plagued your mind, because they left without so much as goodbye.

So, with my mind open, I sit here hoping the answers will follow my praying. All come with a hello, sooner or later they go, and some go without even saying.

Foreign Purchase

The INS officer said something that made me swallow hard.
He said my husband only said I do in order to acquire a green card.
I say, oh my God please let him be wrong.
For my desire was for a union that would be lifelong.
He also exclaimed, and I thought it was funny.
He said that immigrants marry Americans and pay them money
He threatened I could lose my job; even be prosecuted if I did not tell the truth.
But the burden was on him to produce the proof.
He can save himself the trouble, his case can never be made.
Why I will just have to confess that it was the alien who got paid.

A Friend You Doubt

I traveled to a foreign land with a girl I thought was my friend
It was halfway through a three-week tour that the facade came to an end
We made it through Holland, Switzerland and stormed the weather in Germany
But I didn't think I could ever forgive her, after she pulled what she did in Italy
We had spent an absolutely, wonderful day in sunny downtown Rome
She took off with three total strangers that night; I was left stranded and all alone
All I had were my traveler's checks, but they were completely worthless
The hotels were open at that hour, exchanged currency, but they didn't accept American Express
How could I get my hands on some liras without committing a crime?
I felt the weight of the world on my shoulders, and I was running out of time
The banks were closed till the morning, and I didn't know the way to the hotel
I was tired and very scared; not to mention angry as hell
I stumbled across a police station, thinking now I have the upper hand
Before I could even spit out my problem, they said English was a language they did not understand
The despair was more than I could bear, and I could feel my eyes were about to mist
When suddenly a woman emerged from the police station, she said, "I speak English. Is there something I could help you with?"
I explained my dilemma to her, she listened empathetically
What happened next, you would have never guessed, it came as a surprise to me
She hailed a taxicab and bid me to get inside

A Friend You Doubt

The driver was told the destination, then she asked how much for the ride
Then, without a second thought she proceeded to pay the man
I don't know who came out ahead, but I put a twenty-dollar travelers check in her hand
When I arrived and entered my room, my enemy looked me in the eyes
She claimed everything was a misunderstanding, but her words were merely a bunch of lies
It took every ounce of strength I had not to give her a taste of my frustration
I feared if I put my hands on her, I would have found myself getting a ride back to that police station
From that point on I held my peace, to me she didn't even exist
We spent the remainder of our vacation carrying on like this
She had a miserable time and told everyone I was to blame
I had so much fun, had it made in the sun and never even mentioned her name

You Are Not My Friend

You are not my friend.
I don't lie to you.
No matter what you say,
Chances are it didn't go that way.
If you could only open your mouth for the truth,
I swear your tongue would never get loose.

You are not my friend.
I never stole anything from you.
Something would disappear.
I'd thought I lost it.
But it turned out that you took it out of my closet.
I was robbed blind. The thief right in my face.
Girlfriend by the way, how did you get into my safe?

You are not my friend.
You slept with my potential new man.
He said everything he had he would give to me.
I got nothing. You got HIV.

So, you say that you could use a friend like me now.
And that you would make up for the past somehow.
Well honey I will have to think about your news.
And for your information, a friend is to be loved not used.

Introduction To Bluntisms

Introduction To Bluntisms

1. If you neglect to divorce your past, you remain separated from your future.
2. Love people enough and make them tough – be too sweet and you can turn people weak.
3. You say it's love. I say a sorry excuse. It feels more like neglect or some other form of abuse.
4. People know more than they need to, but don't know nearly half of what they should know.
5. When you teach a child authorities should not be mined, that will come back one day to bite many behinds.
6. Check out God one day to avoid checking in hell one night.
7. No, I don't have any sense---you know how much they want for that stuff?
8. I am what I eat, and pudding is always pudding me to sleep.
9. Only sow what you want to see grow.
10. S. I. N. (Situations Involving Negativity)
11. Don't tell me what to write and don't tell me what to think and for the love of God, don't tell me my opinion's wrong because I think your opinion stinks.
12. I'd rather have you mad at me for telling you the truth than to be a hypocrite trying to flatter you so we could be demon buddies.
13. Distraction takes two "I's" Destruction one "U"
14. I give information on a need-to-know basis. If you don't need to know, then I don't need to tell you.
15. It is always good to know the rules of the game, otherwise you will be in a position to be ruled and played.

16. People think you owe them; just because you know them.
17. Goats are headed for disaster; lambs are being steered toward greener pastures.
18. I think I can state confidently, there are more people on the planet who would love to be me; than there are in this world that I'd care to be.
19. Just because you know how to talk, doesn't mean you know what you are talking about.
20. Have no fear when nothing is near. That's when everything sees your need and will appear.
21. This ain't sarcasm baby, it's bluntism – don't get it twisted.
22. You can have it all without the noise or you can have nothing but the noise.
23. Food made to disappear fast are for people who want to do the same.
24. Bertha Blunt fashion line–"POPPA-ROT-Z" READY WEAR
25. Idle words are spoken in vain, so say what you mean and make it plain.
26. People going places are people hard to catch; people going nowhere are not people I'd want to snatch.
27. You must have slipped out your CRACKED mind.
28. The pain gain game – and let the pain begin. A game where pain gauges the gain and every loser can win.
29. I know tens of dozens of people and honestly, I kid you not if they experienced a positive thought, their poor little brains would slip off into the land of shock.
30. You don't know when to take me seriously? Let me help you with that – Seriously, I'm not yours to take.
31. While you are judging me by the skin, I'm in, you need to repent and come out of that sin you in.
32. It is hard to give a helping hand to someone massaging Satan's foot.
33. I'm not sitting around on my duty free; parked and idling for hours in front of the TV... wishing and dreaming that all I could want or ever be would be drug to my front door and handed to me.
34. I've got peace like a river and if it decided its banks want to overflow, I'm gonna be stupid enough to stand back and watch it go.

35. Look I am not rushing into anything I don't want to rush out of.
36. If you don't want to wait for something great, you'll be the one crying when it's too late.
37. Yes, I see your shoulders. All decked out with your behind. And if it ever needs a good dusting, your lips will always be closer than mine.

FIRST AND FOREMOST, I want to thank my Higher Power for my life and the opportunity to share this gift of poetry.
I also would like to thank my many teachers over the years who, not only encouraged me to read and write, but instilled in me a hunger and thirst to be a lifetime learner.

Additionally, I would like to thank all my friends who would listen to my poems and ask me, when was I going to publish my work. I would like to mention a few of them by name: Willie Mae Spencer, Rita Hoffman, Virgia Phoenix, Regina Di Lella, Phyllis Brazee and others. I am grateful for all the friends who believe in me and my works.

www.ingramcontent.com/pod-product-compliance
Ingram Content Group UK Ltd.
Pitfield, Milton Keynes, MK11 3LW, UK
UKHW022220230426
12048UKWH00016BA/964